NEW TECHNOLOGY

environmental technology

Andrew Solway

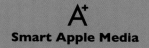

A+

Smart Apple Media

This book has been published in cooperation with Evans Publishing Group.

© Evans Brothers Limited 2008
This edition published under license from Evans Brothers Limited.

Published in the United States by
Smart Apple Media, an imprint of
Black Rabbit Books
P.O. Box 3263, Mankato, Minnesota 56002

Printed in China

Library of Congress Cataloging-in-Publication Data

Solway, Andrew.
     Environmental technology / Andrew Solway.
       p. cm.—(Smart Apple Media. New technology)
     Summary: "Describes new technologies that can help us reduce pollution and global warming, such as alternative energy sources, buildings that cost less to heat, reducing waste, reducing threats to endangered species, and combining all of these to promote sustainable living"—Provided by publisher.
     Includes bibliographical references and index.
     ISBN 978-1-59920-163-4
     1. Pollution—Juvenile literature.
2. Pollution prevention—Juvenile literature.
3. Environmental protection—Juvenile literature. I. Title.
TD176.S64 2009
628—dc22
                                    2008000437

Credits
Series Editor: Paul Humphrey
Editor: Gianna Williams
Designer: Keith Williams
Production: Jenny Mulvanny
Picture researchers: Rachel Tisdale
     and Laura Embriaco

Acknowledgements
Title page: Reuters/Corbis; p.6 Benjamin Lowy/Corbis; p.8 Paul Schraub/ www.calfeedesign.com; p.9 Ramin Talaie/Corbis; p.10 Matej Pribelsky/ istockphoto.com; p.11 Sanyo; p.12 Cree Lighting/NREL; p.13 Jim Sulley/Newscast; p.14: Concordia Language Villages; p.15 Lawrence Berkeley National Laboratory; p.16 ARUP; p.17 Ed Parker/EASI-Images/ CFW Images; p.18 SOM/Crystal CG; p.19 BioRegional; p.20 Rob Hill/ istockphoto.com; p.21 moodboard/Corbis p.22 James Holmes/ZEDCOR/Science Photo Library; p.23 Herbert Kehrer/Zefa/Corbis; p.24 www.iomguide.com; p.26 Solar Sailor Holdings Ltd; p.27 Marine Current Turbines Ltd; p.28 Peter Foerster/Epa/Corbis; p.30 CropEnergies AG; p.31 Hans-Juergen Wege/Epa/Corbis; p.32 Jim Jurica/ istockphoto.com; p.33 Neal Cavalier-Smith/EASI-Images/CFW Images; p.35 Peter Ginter/Science Faction/Getty Images; p.36 Reuters/Corbis; p.37 Walter Meayers Edwards/National Geographic/Getty Images; p.38 Scott Olson/Getty Images; p.39 Sarah Leen/National Geographic/Getty Images; p.40 Paulo Fridman/Corbis; p.41 Foster & Partners; p.42 Mark Ralston/AFP/Getty Images; p.43 Arctic-Images/Corbis.

contents

introduction

Today, the world is in danger. Scientists and leaders from most countries agree—if we don't do something soon, our planet will become unfit to live on. The biggest threat is global warming.

Can we save the world? The Earth is warming up, mainly because of the greenhouse gases that are released into the air whenever we burn fossil fuels (coal, oil, or gas). We burn fossil fuels to get energy. Every time we turn on the furnace, make coffee, or drive a car, we are using energy, and most of this energy comes from fossil fuels.

At an oil refinery in Libya, waste gases are burned off as flares. Flaring burns as much gas each year as France and Germany use. This produces large amounts of carbon dioxide, so some refineries now remove waste gas in other ways.

CARBON DIOXIDE

Coal, oil, and gas are made mostly from carbon. When they burn, the main gas that is produced is carbon dioxide. Each year, we release millions of tons of carbon dioxide into the atmosphere. This is the main cause of global warming.

Direct sunlight

Some infrared radiation escapes into space

Carbon dioxide in atmosphere absorbs infrared radiation

Some infrared radiation warms atmosphere

Sunlight is absorbed by the Earth, then released as infrared radiation (heat)

Carbon dioxide creates global warming because it stops infrared radiation from escaping into space.

To slow global warming, we need to reduce the amount of fossil fuels we use. How can we do this? Environmental technology can help.

How can technology help? Any kind of technology that helps reduce our impact on the planet is called environmental technology. It can be as simple as a cooking fire that uses less fuel, or as complicated as a satellite in space collecting the sun's energy. Environmental technology can work in several different ways. It can help us to use less energy, for instance, by making more efficient machines and buildings.

Cutting pollution Global warming is not the only threat to our planet.

Pollution is another problem. It can affect people as well as other living things. Pollution can be caused by things that we throw away, waste products from factories, or even chemicals used by farmers. These substances can pollute the air, the land, rivers and streams, or even the sea.

Environmental technology can also help reduce pollution. In some areas it has already helped, but we could reduce pollution much more if environmental technology were used more widely. Environmental technology can help us find sources of energy that do not cause pollution or global warming. We can also use technology to help cut down on waste or to find uses for waste materials.

CHAPTER 1
saving energy

One way we can stop burning so much fossil fuel is to use less energy. People in developed countries use a lot of energy. They use energy to heat or cool their homes, for cars, computers, refrigerators, washing machines, and many other things.

It also takes energy to make all the products we use. In contrast, countries in the developing world use much less energy. If every country in the world used energy at the same rate as the United Kingdom (UK), we would need the resources of three planets to keep us going. If we all used energy at the same rate as the U.S., we would need 30 planets.

We can save energy in very simple ways, for instance, by turning the heating or the air conditioning down, or traveling by bike, bus, or train instead of in a car. However, we can only make limited savings this way. Environmental technology can help us make other energy savings, by making the machines and other devices we use more efficient.

Saving energy can be as simple as riding a bike instead of driving a car. If you ride a bamboo bike, even better—it's biodegradable as well as carbon free.

More efficient cars Of all the machines that we use in our everyday lives, cars and other vehicles use the most energy. However, they are not very efficient. Only about 15 percent of the energy in a car's fuel is used to move the car or work the lights or the heating. The rest of the energy is lost, mostly as heat.

More than half the wasted energy is lost in the engine. Gasoline and diesel engines work by burning a mix of fuel and air. They cannot work without producing heat, but this heat is wasted energy. Carefully controlling the fuel and air mix in the cylinders can make the engine more efficient. A turbocharger also helps get more energy from an engine. A turbocharger uses a fan to push more air into the engine cylinders, and this increases the power of the engine. Many cars already have fuel control and turbochargers.

Hybrid vehicles, such as this bus, run on two power sources—a traditional engine and an electric motor—in order to use less fuel.

Engines also waste quite a lot of fuel when they are idling, for instance, when a vehicle is waiting at traffic lights. A new way to cut down these losses is to use an integrated starter generator, or ISG. This is a system that turns the engine off when a car stops, then automatically

WHAT'S NEXT?

Cars of the future could be powered by fuel cells and electric motors, instead of gasoline or diesel engines. Fuel cells are like powerful batteries, but they make electricity using a fuel such as hydrogen gas or methanol, so they don't have to be recharged. Electric motors and fuel cells are far more efficient than normal car engines. Some fuel cell cars are being built now, but they are expensive. There is also the problem that hydrogen and methanol are usually made from fossil fuels. However, in the next 20 years or so, we should be able to solve these problems.

starts it again as you press on the accelerator to pull away. The ISG also saves energy in another way. Most cars use brakes that rely on friction to slow the car down, and the braking process wastes energy. An ISG uses a different braking system that actually produces energy by generating electricity.

The best way to improve the efficiency of vehicles would be to change the way they are powered. An electric motor, for instance, uses energy much more efficiently than a normal car engine. It would also help reduce global warming if cars used nonfossil fuels. Both these ideas are discussed in Chapter 4.

Turning your TV off with the remote leaves it on standby, which means it uses electricity even while you are not using it.

Energy-efficient machines Walk around your house and count how many devices there are that use electricity or some other kind of energy. The biggest energy users are heating and air conditioning. Other devices include lights, washing machines, stoves, refrigerators, vacuum cleaners, computers, TVs, and radios.

STANDBY POWER

For electronic devices such as TVs and computers, the biggest waste of energy is when a device is on standby. It is using electricity even when it is turned off. Most devices on standby use only 10–15 watts of power, but there are millions of them. In most countries, standby power uses between 5 and 10 percent of household electricity. In Australia and Japan, it is even higher, at 12 to 13 percent. In the U.S., standby power costs about $4 billion each year and produces 29 million tons (27 million t) of CO_2. In the UK, electronic equipment on standby produces a total of 3.4 million tons (3.1 million t) of CO_2, at a cost of over $985 million. If a million PC users unplugged their computers when they turned them off, it would save the equivalent of 66,000 gallons (250,000 L) of gasoline.

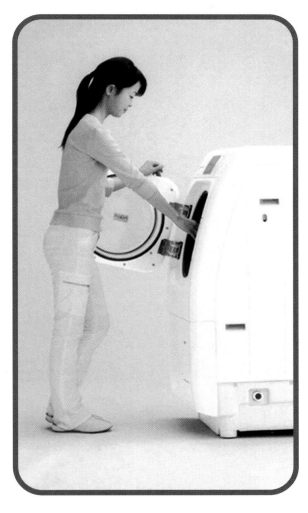

New "air" washing machines like this one use ozone (an "active" kind of oxygen) to clean clothes. Avoiding wetting and drying clothes when cleaning them saves a lot of energy.

WHAT'S NEXT?

As global warming increases, many more places in the world will have limited water supplies. Energy-saving washing machines and dishwashers are therefore designed to use less water as well as less energy. A new washing machine design from two Singapore students could make it possible to wash clothes without using water at all! The Air Wash washing machine uses negative ions and highly pressurized air to clean clothes without using any water. The designers are currently working on turning their design into a practical machine.

The biggest electricity users are in the kitchen and laundry room. Washing machines, dryers, and stoves use a lot of electricity, while refrigerators use less energy but have to remain on all the time. The best modern appliances use far less energy than in the past. Modern refrigerator-freezers, for instance, use less than a third of the energy of similar units built 30 years ago. New washing machines that use a combination of steam and water spray for washing use less energy. The clothes are much drier at the end of the washing cycle, which saves energy if the clothes are then dried in a dryer. However, there are a lot more of these machines in use now than 30 years ago.

Smart buildings We are often told to turn off lights, or use less heating to save energy. However, it's easy to forget to do these things. What if it could all happen automatically?

Most buildings have some kind of automatic control over the heating and air conditioning. For instance, your house may have a timer system for central heating. Some offices and other large buildings have building management systems. These are computer systems that control the hot water, heating, air conditioning, and sometimes the lights and ventilation, too.

Most building management systems are not very flexible. They might be set up to keep all the offices in a building, or a section of a building, at a particular temperature during the day, or at the times when people are working there. However, a few buildings have better systems that are more flexible. For instance, the system in a hotel can be given the timetable of room bookings, and it will then make sure that each room is at the right temperature when people want to use it. A good building management system can save up to 30 percent of the energy costs for a building.

More light, less heat LEDs (light-emitting diodes) are lights made using semiconductors (the materials used in microchips). LEDs glow at much lower

Low-energy fluorescent lightbulbs are already replacing conventional ones. By 2010, LED lights like this could be replacing fluorescent lights.

WHAT'S NEXT?

Within 10 years, new homes could be fitted with "intelligent" building management systems. The system would control the heating, air conditioning, and ventilation so that rooms in use are kept at a particular temperature. It would also be flexible enough to allow people to open windows or turn on the heat if they are too warm or too cold. Sensors would detect when someone goes into a room, turn on the lights if needed, and perhaps turn up the heat. The system could use weather forecast information to plan ahead, for instance, by turning on the heat earlier on mornings when cold weather is forecast.

temperatures than ordinary lightbulbs. This means they are more efficient and use less power than lightbulbs. They also last a long time. Improvements in LED lighting have already led to LED flashlights and car lights. By 2010, we will have LEDs that are as powerful and efficient as the best kinds of lightbulb. They will be used for house

This eye-catching lighting display in Jacksonville, Florida, is an impressive advertisement for LED lighting.

lighting, streetlights, and many other applications. As well as being more efficient, they use less energy when they are turned on and off. They are also very thin, and in the future they may also be flexible.

CHAPTER 2
improving buildings

In the developed world, buildings account for over half the total amount of energy that we use. They also produce over half of all greenhouse gases that contribute to global warming. A large part of this energy is used to heat buildings when the weather is cold, or cool them when it is hot. However, with the right design and modern technology, it is quite possible to cut the energy costs of a house or another building to practically nothing.

Planning for low energy Making a low-energy building needs planning and design. A lot depends on what the climate is like. In a hot climate, the design needs to focus on keeping the building cool. This usually means small windows and thick, insulating walls on the side that gets the most sun, and a good air-circulation system to draw out hot air and draw in cooler air. In a cold climate, the focus is on keeping the building warm. The side of the building that gets the most sun should have large windows to make the most of the sunlight, and there should be good insulation to stop heat from escaping. Methods of heating and cooling that make use of the natural climate in this way are known as passive design. Over 6,000 passive houses have been built in Germany and the Netherlands. In 2006, a German language center called the Waldsee BioHaus was built in Minneapolis, Minnesota, using passive

design ideas. The BioHaus uses 85 percent less energy than an ordinary building.

Planning the landscape can also be part of passive design. Trees and other plants improve air quality. Deciduous trees can provide shade in summer but then allow the sun to warm the

This BioHaus low-energy building in Minnesota is one of the most energy-efficient buildings in the country. It uses 85 percent less energy than most similar U.S. buildings.

building in winter. When the CK Choi building in British Columbia, Canada, was built, existing trees on the site were saved, and many gingko trees were planted. Trees like gingkoes are especially good at cleaning the air of pollutants.

E glass If a building has good insulation, this saves a lot of energy. The building will need very little energy to keep it cool in summer and warm in winter. The parts of a building that are least insulated are the windows, because ordinary glass is not a good insulator. Low-energy buildings use new kinds of glass known as low-E glass. The glass has special coatings that reflect heat back from the surface instead of letting it through. Low-E glass can be combined with double or even triple glazing, with special gases such as argon between the layers of glass. Windows made this way are five times better at insulating than ordinary double glazing.

Some low-energy houses use windows in other ways. They are used as part of a smart building management system. Computers control the way that windows open and close, and

These windows at a research laboratory in the U.S. are photochromic. This means that when the sun is bright, the windows darken to stop the inside of the building from heating up too much.

WHAT'S NEXT?

It may take 20 years, but two new kinds of material could revolutionize windows in the future. Transparent insulating materials (TIMs) are as clear as glass, but they do not let through heat or cold. They are made from honeycombs or plastic "aerogels" (materials with billions of tiny air bubbles trapped inside).

Electrochromic windows have a coating that darkens when electricity passes through it. Electrochromic windows controlled by a computer could change automatically to cut down sunlight in hot weather and let it in when it is cold.

shutters cover the windows at certain times. These controls are part of a system that keeps the building at a comfortable temperature.

Changing the air If a building is drafty, no amount of insulation will keep it warm in winter and cool in summer. However, if a building is completely sealed, the air becomes stuffy and unpleasant. So in a low-energy building, the ventilation has to be carefully controlled. One way of doing this is to use heat exchangers. These are machines that swap heat between air coming into a building and air flowing out. If it is cold outside, the heat exchanger uses heat from air as it leaves the building to warm up cold air coming in.

The Eastgate office block in Harare, Zimbabwe, cools itself without air conditioning. During the day, the building absorbs the sun's heat, keeping the inside cool. At night ventilation cools the building down again.

HOW IT WORKS

The Eastgate in Harare, Zimbabwe, is an office block which uses a special ventilation system to naturally cool the building. Some of the ideas for the building came from studies of termite mounds. Some kinds of termites live in large colonies in tall mounds. The inside of the mound stays at a constant temperature, even though it is hot by day and cold at night.

The Eastgate designers learned from the termites. During the day when it is hot, the thick walls of the building help keep out the heat. As air inside the building warms up, it rises and is let out through special chimneys on the roof. Cooler air is drawn in at ground level. In the cool of the night, the warm walls of the building give out their heat, and it is drawn out through the roof chimneys by fans.

Another way to help keep a building cool and ventilated in warm climates is to have an air space underground. Underground, the temperature is little affected by the temperature at the surface. It is cooler in summer and warmer in winter. If air from a building is circulated through an underground space, the air will be warmed in winter and cooled in summer.

Extra energy Even the best low-energy buildings need some energy for things like heating water and running the electric lights. This energy often comes from solar power.

There are two kinds of solar power. Solar thermal power uses the heat of the sun to warm up water. This is ideal for heating the water supply. Photovoltaic power is converting sunlight into electricity. Photovoltaic panels are quite expensive, and they do not produce that much power. However, an array of 20–40 panels can supply enough electricity for a house. Today it is possible to get photovoltaic roof tiles, wall panels, and even "glass" that can turn sunlight into electricity.

Mud, straw, and newspaper Some materials need more energy to make them than others. An aluminum pan, for instance, has to be made from its raw material (bauxite), a process that uses huge amounts of electricity. More energy is needed to transport the aluminum to a saucepan factory and to turn the aluminum into a pan. The total amount of energy involved in producing an object or a material is called its "embodied energy."

Solar panels on the roof produce most of the energy for this sheltered housing in the UK.

WHAT'S NEXT?

The Pearl River Tower is a zero-energy skyscraper being built in the city of Dongtan in China (it will be finished in 2010). The designers plan to take advantage of the height of the tower to generate electricity. At two levels, there will be openings right through the building. The openings are shaped to draw in air, which rushes through a bank of wind turbines. Because they are in special "wind tunnels," the turbines will generate 15 times more energy than if they were free-standing.

Using building materials with low embodied energy is a good way to save energy. You can build a house from low-energy materials such as mud, straw, and old newspapers. Using recycled building materials, such as old bricks or wooden flooring, uses 95 percent less energy than making new ones.

Rammed earth construction (see panel below) is basically making walls out of

HOW IT WORKS

Rammed earth construction is a modern take on an ancient method. Earth taken from a building site is moistened with water to make a thick mud. This is then mixed with a small amount of cement. The mixture is then rammed into wooden molds or forms. Once the walls are finished and dry, they are strong and weatherproof, but with much lower embodied energy than concrete walls. Rammed earth construction is used for houses in many warm climates, including the southern U.S., Australia, and New Zealand.

Pearl River Tower is a "green" skyscraper currently being built in Dongtan, China. This artist's drawing shows the two levels where air will blow right through the skyscraper to generate wind power.

mud. Mud, or adobe, has been used in this way for many years. However, new techniques mean that the material is far more weatherproof and long lasting. Another new low-energy material is a kind of concrete made from lime and hemp. The material is as strong as concrete, but has the advantage that it allows water vapor to escape. This helps prevent dampness. Low-energy material can also be used for insulation or for floor and wall coverings. One new kind of low-energy insulating material is made from waste newspaper. The material is injected into cavities in walls or into roof spaces by a special machine, which blows air into it and "fluffs it up." The trapped air makes it an excellent insulator as long as it is kept dry.

How much energy can we save?

Architects who design low-energy buildings combine many different methods for reducing energy use. Because they often use natural materials and make use of sunlight and natural ventilation, low-energy buildings are usually pleasant places to live or work.

Even limited design changes can make major energy savings. A low-energy home, using passive design, can cut energy use by about 85 percent, compared with a typical modern house. With the addition of devices such as solar panels and wind turbines, a

building can be "zero-energy" (it needs no electricity or heating). The Beddington Zero-Energy Development (BedZED) is a group of houses and apartments in London, England, that do not need outside energy for heating, lighting, and power. The buildings are designed to make the most of the sun's energy. They are superinsulated and get water heating and electricity from solar panels. Brightly colored chimneys are ventilators and heat exchangers. Warm, stale air going out of the chimneys heats up the cool air coming in.

Solar panels and colorful rotating chimneys on the roof of the Beddington Zero-Energy Development (BedZED) in London

CHAPTER 3
too much waste

As well as using energy, the way that people live in developed countries produces a lot of waste. At home, we throw away waste food, the packaging from things we buy, old clothes, old shoes, and even old TVs and furniture.

Offices throw away tons of paper; builders throw out all kinds of building waste. Factories may have waste materials such as metal or plastic scraps. They may also produce waste chemicals, some of which can be toxic.

The total amount of waste we produce is staggering. In a year, the European Union produces 1,141 pounds (518 kg) of waste per person. The U.S. produces about 12 billion tons (11 billion t) of waste

Across Europe and the United States, the amount of waste dumped in landfill sites like this one is falling, thanks to public awareness about recycling and greater concern for the environment.

WHAT'S NEXT?

Researchers in Cambridge, UK, are investigating the possibility of making a machine that recycles waste paper on the spot in an office. A large proportion of paper thrown away in offices is waste photocopying or paper that is creased or torn. The machine would remove photocopying toner from the paper, add water, turn it into a thick paste, then make the paper paste into new sheets.

annually: that's about seven garbage trucks of waste for every person in the country. Most of this waste material is dumped: it may either go into a landfill site, or it may be incinerated (burned), or it might be dumped at sea.

To deal with waste in the best way, we need to reduce the amount of waste we produce, reuse as much of the waste that we cannot avoid producing, and recover materials or energy from what is left.

Less packaging Many things we buy are overpackaged. If we cut down on the packaging we use, we avoid huge amounts of waste.

Simpler packages that need less material mean less waste. Computer-controlled, precision manufacturing makes it possible to make packages that use far less material than in the past. In France, for example, new wine bottles use 3 ounces (80 g) less glass than in the past, saving 55,000 tons (50,000 t) of glass annually.

WHAT'S NEXT?

One way to get rid of packaging is to eat it! New kinds of packaging are being developed that are edible. Some of these are tasteless coatings that protect food from spoiling and can be eaten along with the food. Others are edible wrappings, made from fruit or vegetable purée, which can add to the taste of the food.

Another way to cut down waste is to use recycled materials for packaging. Amber or blue glass jars look attractive and can be made using over 60 percent recycled glass. Supermarkets are beginning to try out recycled paper and plastic for packaging fresh fruit and vegetables, and some milk bottles are now being made from recycled plastic.

People in many countries have now become accustomed to recycling plastic bottles.

recycle

Another possibility is to use packages that are biodegradable (they break down fairly quickly). Paper and cardboard are biodegradable; these materials can be included in compost. Most traditional plastics are almost indestructible, but recently biodegradable plastics have been developed, though sometimes this means that the plastic simply breaks up into smaller pieces of plastic. Some of these new plastics are made from plant materials. Over time, they break down and become part of the soil when they are buried in the ground.

Recovering waste If we do have to throw things away, we can often recover some of the materials by recycling. Many countries now recycle metals, paper, and glass. This reduces the number of bottles, cans, and newspapers going into landfill sites. However, recycling plastics is less successful. Some plastics can be recycled. PET plastic, for example, which is used for plastic bottles, can now be recycled, and recycled PET bottles are already being used. Researchers are now working on finding ways to recycle plastics such as PVC, and items that contain a mixture of plastics.

WHAT'S NEXT?

The best plant plastics developed so far are called "polylactides" (PLAs). They are made from a simple chemical called lactic acid, which can be made by breaking down plant extracts with bacteria. Another kind of "natural" plastic, PHA, is made directly as tiny granules in some kinds of bacteria.

In the future, it may be possible to "engineer" plants to produce plastics directly. For example, plants such as potatoes and cereals produce large amounts of starch for food storage. However, by adding bacterial genes, they could be made to produce PLA or other plastics instead. Scientists have already engineered corn plants that can make PLA. In the future we may be able to "grow" a whole range of plastics this way.

This plastic sheeting is produced from recycled waste plastic. It is widely used in construction work.

Waste paper ready for recycling outside a recycled paper plant

Waste food (but not cooked food or meat) and garden waste can be recycled by composting it. Paper and cardboard can be included in compost, too. People have made compost in their gardens for many years. However, in many places, local organizations now collect kitchen and garden waste for composting on a large scale. New methods of "hot composting" can produce good compost in a few weeks. The compost can be sold to gardeners to improve the soil in their gardens. Another way of dealing with kitchen waste that is being tested is by biodigestion. This is similar to composting, but the process is quicker and produces two products: biogas, which can be burned for energy, and a liquid residue that can be used as a fertilizer on farmland, if it has been carefully treated to get rid of harmful bacteria.

Building with waste New materials are being developed that are made from waste. One kind of material, made from a mixture of crushed glass, ash, and bitumen (tar), could be used to replace blocks of concrete. Researchers are also finding uses for rubber from old tires. Researchers in the UK have produced a material made from recycled tires that can be used for roof tiles. Others in Australia have developed a new way of mixing recycled rubber with new rubber that produces much better quality rubber than in the past.

Energy from waste Even the waste left after reusing and recovering as much material as possible can be put to some use. One way to deal with it is incineration (burning it). This produces heat, which can be used for heating or to produce electricity. Incineration also reduces the waste to ash, which takes up far less space in landfills than other waste. Burning waste produces polluting gases, but

This incinerator on the Isle of Man burns waste to produce electricity. Unlike many incinerators, this one produces very clean energy. It releases only steam into the atmosphere.

WHAT'S NEXT?

Metals were the first materials to be recycled, and metal recycling is the most successful. Scrap metals are first chopped up into smaller pieces, and then different metals are separated. Ferrous metals (iron and steel) can be separated from nonferrous ones using magnets. Other metals have different densities, and these differences can be used to sort them. Once the different kinds of metal have been separated, they can be reused. Often the recycled metal is mixed with newly produced metal.

A new kind of recycling technique that might be used in the future is cold bonding. Researchers at the University of Cambridge in the UK have found that scraps of aluminum or other metals can be joined to make new material by pressing them together. Cold bonding uses far less energy than other types of recycling. We may start seeing cold-bonded materials in the next five years.

modern incinerators remove these pollutants from the waste gas. Incinerating materials such as plastics also produces carbon dioxide, which adds to the global warming problem.

A better way of getting energy from waste is by gasification. The waste is heated in a low-oxygen atmosphere and produces a gas that can be used as a fuel. This way of dealing with waste is still in the research stage. Test gasifier plants have been built in Japan and Germany, and a plant designed to burn 9,900 tons (9,000 t) of waste a year is being built in the UK.

Dealing with sewage Cleaning up the vast amounts of sewage that cities produce is as big a headache as getting rid of other waste. Removing sewage also uses large amounts of water. Some low-energy buildings have found ways

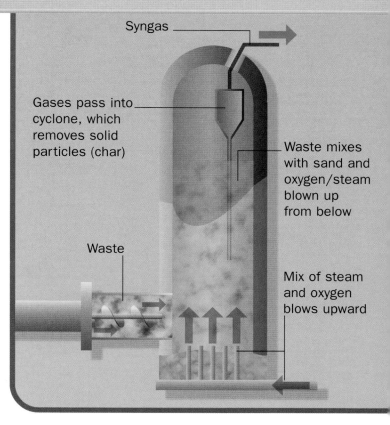

There are several ways of gasifying waste. In this method (fluidized-bed gasification), the waste is heated by a mixture of high-temperature steam and oxygen, which is blown up through a bed of sand. It produces a gas called syngas, which is mostly hydrogen.

to deal with their own sewage. The CK Choi Building in Canada has omposting toilets that reduce water use by about 260 gal (1,000 L) per day. The compost produced is rich in nitrogen and makes an excellent fertilizer. Other dirty water is cleaned in special trenches containing reeds and other plants. These artificial reed beds make the water clean enough to swim in. The cleaned water is actually used for watering the gardens around the building.

WHAT'S NEXT?

Scientists have discovered that it is possible to use bacteria to generate electricity. This amazing discovery is very exciting, because bacteria can live on all kinds of food, including waste material. In the future, it may be possible to generate electricity using bacteria fed on city garbage or farm waste.

CHAPTER 4
new energy sources

No matter how well we conserve energy and reduce waste, we will still need large amounts of energy in the future. If we can get less of this energy from fossil fuels, it will help cut down on pollution and global warming, thereby reducing damage to the environment.

One of the biggest areas of environmental technology is research into finding other energy sources that do not cause pollution and don't release large amounts of carbon dioxide into the atmosphere. To be useful, the source needs to be cheap, practical, and able to supply large amounts of energy.

Water power Hydroelectricity is electricity produced by harnessing the power of running water. Today, countries such as Norway and Paraguay get nearly all their electricity from

WHAT'S NEXT?

Scientists and car manufacturers are developing many new ways of powering cars. Hybrid cars, which use a combination of a normal engine and electric batteries, are already being produced. There are also a few cars that run on biofuel, and dual-fuel cars that can use either biofuel or ordinary fuel. Some buses and trains run on hydrogen gas. Hydrogen produces only water (steam) when it burns. At sea, new kinds of boats which are partly solar powered or sail powered can save a lot of fuel and cut down on carbon dioxide emissions.

The Solar Sailor *is a ferryboat in Sydney Harbor, Australia. It is a hybrid boat, powered partly by solar panels and partly by a diesel engine.*

hydropower. However, producing lots more hydroelectricity is not so simple. Some countries have no large, fast-flowing rivers suitable for hydroelectric power stations. Building dams for hydroelectric energy production can also damage river wildlife. In other countries, all the best hydropower sites are already being used.

One way we can get more energy from water is to use small power plants, or "microhydro." These kinds of plants could be set up in many more places, to supply a small area or even just one house.

Tidal power is a way of getting power from the ocean rather than from rivers. A few tidal power stations have been built, but there are a limited number of places where the change in tide is large enough to produce large amounts of electricity. However, we may soon be able to get energy from the tides in another way, using tidal stream generators. These are underwater propellers that get energy from the movement of water in a similar way to windmills in the air. The world's first tidal stream generator is currently being built off the coast of Northern Ireland. The generator uses two huge, 52-ft (16-m) propellers to generate electricity from the tide. A larger generator using five propellers is planned for the Bristol Channel, UK.

The first large-scale tidal stream generator is being built on the coast of Northern Ireland. This artist's drawing shows how the generator will look.

Solar power We have already seen that photovoltaic cells (solar cells) can be used to produce electricity for houses. However, at present they are not used for generating electricity on a large scale. There are several reasons for this. First, solar cells are not very efficient. Most only turn about 12 to 16 percent of the light that falls on them into electricity. Second, solar cells only work during daylight hours, and they work best in strong sunlight. Third, solar cells are expensive to produce. However, some new kinds of solar cells promise to be much more efficient and perhaps cheaper to make. These new cells have a coating of nanocrystals (a very pure layer of crystals just one molecule thick),

WHAT'S NEXT?

A small-scale source of power for the future could be solar-powered clothing! Flexible solar panels now being tested could eventually be made into sun-powered fabrics. You could recharge your phone or power your music player by putting it in your pocket.

which greatly improves the ability of the solar cell to collect energy. Solar cells made this way could be in use within 5 or 10 years.

Solar collectors, which concentrate the heat of the sun, are another kind of

This solar power station in eastern Germany produces power for a small village. Banks of solar panels collect the sun's energy and turn it into electricity.

solar power. A few small power stations use this kind of power to produce electricity. However, such power stations can only work during the day, and they are limited to warm areas.

Wind power Modern wind turbines can produce cheap electricity from the energy in moving air. In the near future, the amount of wind energy produced will increase, as offshore wind farms begin operating. These are groups of wind turbines built in places offshore where there are strong winds. However, wind farms can only replace a small amount of the energy produced by fossil-fuel power stations, and they only work well where the wind blows strongly for most of the year.

An idea for future wind power is to build "flying windmills." Scientists in San Diego are developing flying wind

generators designed to work in the high-speed winds of the jet stream, about 6 miles (11 km) above the Earth. The first full-scale generator should be ready to test in about five years.

Nuclear power Nuclear power stations seem like an ideal alternative to fossil fuels. They are efficient, they produce no greenhouse gases, and they can make large amounts of electricity from small amounts of fuel. The technology of nuclear power stations has been tested around the world. However, nuclear power stations are very expensive to build, so they need to run for a long time

A prototype design for wind generators in the jet stream, high in the air. As the wind turbines spin, they work like helicopter blades to keep the generator flying, as well as producing electricity. The electricity from the wind turbines travels to earth down the tether (a wire connecting the turbines to the ground).

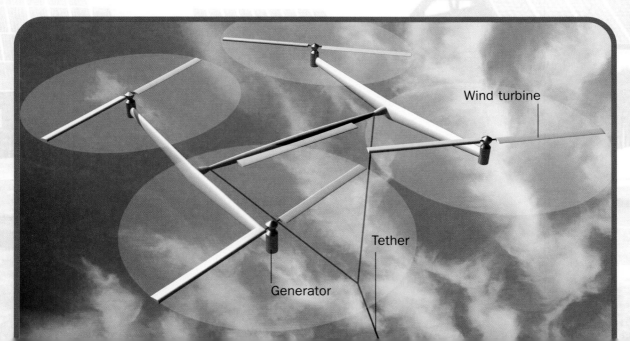

Wind turbine

Tether

Generator

to be worth building. Waste fuel from a nuclear power station is radioactive, and it stays dangerous for hundreds of years. No one has yet found a good way to keep the fuel safe until it is no longer radioactive. There is also the risk of nuclear accidents, like the one at Chernobyl in Ukraine, in 1986. In the future, we may get energy from a different kind of nuclear power, called nuclear fusion.

HOW IT WORKS

The incredible amount of energy that the sun produces comes from a process called nuclear fusion. Fusion is fueled by hydrogen gas, which is turned into helium in the process. Scientists in many countries are working on developing nuclear fusion reactors to use on Earth. However, fusion reactors are extremely expensive to build, and as yet they do not produce much energy. One large research reactor in France uses magnetic fields to control the incredibly hot gases involved. Two other research projects, in the U.S. and in the UK, use lasers to compress and heat hydrogen to millions of degrees Celsius. However, none of the projects now underway is likely to produce any results until at least 2020. It could be 50 years or more before we have working fusion reactors.

Biofuels Biofuels are fuels similar to gasoline, diesel, or natural gas, but made from plants. When biofuels are burned, they release carbon dioxide. However, the carbon dioxide does not add to the total amount in the air, because the carbon has not been locked away in the ground for millions of years, as it has in fossil fuels. The plants absorbed the carbon dioxide from the air when they were growing. Burning biofuels only releases that carbon dioxide back into the air again.

A large-scale bioethanol factory in Germany. Each year, the factory turns 770,000 tons (700,000 t) of grain into bioethanol fuel.

WHAT'S NEXT?

Scientists in the U.S. are experimenting with making biofuels from switchgrass. This tall grass grows very quickly, and it will grow on soil that is too poor for food crops. Switchgrass can even restore nutrients to poor soil. It could therefore be grown in rotation with food crops.

Biogas made from waste material is not usually suitable as a fuel for cars. However, at a factory in Jameln, Germany, the biogas is refined (improved) to make car fuel.

Biofuels can be made from many kinds of plants, or even from waste materials. At present, most biofuels are made from crops that could be used as food, such as sugar cane and corn. Making biofuels this way on a large scale could cause serious problems, because land that could be used to grow food would be used instead for fuel production. There is not enough good farmland on Earth to grow enough plants for both food and biofuels. However, other kinds of biofuel are being developed that are made from plants that grow fast and can tolerate poor soil. It is also possible to make biofuels from microorganisms such as algae.

Biogas is a promising kind of biofuel because it can be made from waste materials rather than crops. The gas is made by breaking down animal dung and other kinds of waste material in closed containers called digesters. Bacteria and other microbes in the digester produce the gas. The process is similar to the way that yeasts produce the gases that make bread rise. Small-scale biogas plants are being used successfully in the countryside in India, Sri Lanka, Costa Rica, and other developing countries. In Europe, cities such as Berne, Lille, and Rome have large biogas plants producing fuel for buses. In Sweden, there are over 1,500 biogas-powered vehicles, including a biogas train and 22 biogas filling stations.

CHAPTER 5
protecting the environment

Humans cause damage to the environment in many ways. We cut down forests, plow up grasslands, and drain wetlands to make room for buildings, factories, and farms. The gases released when we burn fossil fuels cause problems such as global warming and acid rain.

Oil refineries, chemical factories, and other kinds of industry produce polluting wastes that get into the air and into water. The fertilizers and pesticides that farmers spray on their fields linger in the soil and wash into rivers and streams, causing more pollution.

Polluted water, like this untreated waste, is a problem in many parts of the world.

The damage to the environment does not just affect humans—it affects other living things, too. According to the latest surveys, one in eight birds and nearly 70 percent of all plants are now threatened with extinction. Most of

WHAT'S NEXT?

In the future, we may be able to reduce global warming using long, hollow pipes suspended in the ocean. The idea is currently being tested by a company in the U.S. Wave motion moves the pipes up and down in the water. When they move downward, colder water from below is forced up the pipe to the surface. A valve stops water from going down the pipe the other way. Colder water from deeper in the ocean is richer in nutrients than water at the surface. This means that more algae and other plant-like creatures can grow in the water, and these absorb more carbon dioxide from the air.

Encontrando a Dios

Nuestra respuesta a
los dones de Dios

Dios

Finding·God

Our Response to God's Gifts

¡NUEVO!

LOYOLA PRESS.
A JESUIT MINISTRY
UN MINISTERIO JESUITA

FindingGod.com
800.621.1008

Tigers are among the most endangered large mammals in the world, despite efforts to protect them over many years. Conservation efforts mostly involve trying to restore polluted or damaged habitats, buying up land for nature reserves, and developing "wildlife corridors" that allow animals to move between areas of protected habitat.

these species are dying out because of the loss of their habitat. Many forests, wetlands, and other natural habitats have been destroyed or damaged. Some animals, especially large predators such as tigers, survive only in small pockets, isolated from each other. How can environmental technology help solve these problems?

Living technology At many old mine and factory sites, the land is contaminated with substances such as arsenic and mercury, or even radioactive substances such as uranium. Cleaning up these

sites properly would be enormously expensive, so they are often abandoned. However, scientists are now finding new ways of cleaning up such sites with the help of living creatures. The process is known as bioremediation.

For example, in 2001 a team of scientists in Florida found that a common kind of fern, originally from China, could take up arsenic from the ground and concentrate it in its fronds. This fern has been used at contaminated sites to help get rid of arsenic.

Other kinds of bioremediation use bacteria and other microbes instead of ferns. In South Carolina, scientists from the U.S. Geological Survey used soil bacteria to remove pollution caused by a massive spillage of jet fuel that had happened some years earlier. Within a year, contamination had been reduced by 75 percent.

WHAT'S NEXT?

Trees are good at cleaning carbon from the air, but one scientist thinks that an artificial tree could do the job better. Dr. Klaus Lackner, based at Columbia University, has invented a synthetic tree that will filter carbon out of the air. An absorbent coating on its slats would capture carbon as the wind blows through them. Dr. Lackner believes that each tree would remove 99,000 tons (90,000 t) of carbon dioxide every year, the equivalent of 15,000 cars. But will people be happy to see forests of artificial trees?

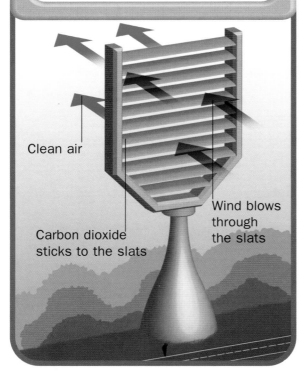

Clean air

Carbon dioxide sticks to the slats

Wind blows through the slats

How Dr. Lackner's synthetic tree would clean the air of carbon dioxide.

Make our own microbes? When scientists discover a useful microbe, they look at its DNA (its genes) to try and find out more about it. In the future, it may be possible to modify the DNA of microbes, for instance, to make them better at cleaning up polluted water or soil. However, people have different opinions about genetically modifying (changing) microbes. Some groups or individuals think it is not safe to change a microbe's genes, because we do not understand enough about the effect this will have. Others think that genetic modification could solve many problems.

FOR AND AGAINST

For
- Artificial microbes could combine the most useful parts of several different microbes found in nature.
- Microbes could be "tailor-made" to clean up oil spills or clean polluted soil.
- They could help us learn more about DNA and genes.

Against
- We do not understand enough about the effects of changing a microbe's genes.
- An artificial microbe that causes disease could be made by accident.

WHAT'S NEXT?

In the future, we could be cleaning up industrial waste with genetically engineered trees. Scientists in Tennessee have discovered that they can add an animal gene to poplar trees which makes the poplar trees get rid of a poisonous chemical called TCE. TCE is a pollutant found at many industrial sites. It will take 10 to 15 years to fully develop this kind of bioremediation. In time, scientists may also engineer other kinds of "clean-up" plants. We will then be able to clean up industrial sites by planting a garden of these plants.

Scientists at the Bayer BioScience laboratory in Potsdam, Germany, use genetic modification techniques to improve crop plants.

Saving species Saving the world's endangered species is an enormous task. All around the world, plant and animal habitats are constantly being destroyed by human activity, such as clearing forest for farmland or for timber, or draining wetlands to build on.

To try to do the most good, scientists have identified "hot spots" that have high biodiversity (many different animal and plant species). These biodiversity hot spots are where people are doing most work to save species.

Saving plants Environmental technology is playing an important part in saving plant species in these hot spots. Often, researchers find only one or two plants of an endangered species, and there may be no flowers or seeds. In these cases, they can grow new plants by a process called "tissue culture." Small pieces of plant material are grown

In a laboratory in Honduras, scientists are trying to save rare orchids by growing thousands of them using tissue culture. These orchids are the national flower of Honduras.

in the laboratory, by giving them food and special substances called "plant hormones," which encourage growth. With luck, the pieces will produce some shoots. Researchers separate these shoots and grow them, using hormones. The shoots grow into normal plants. In one hot spot in the Himalayas, scientists have saved some plants from extinction by growing them this way and then replanting them in their habitat.

Cloning Tissue culture does not work for animals, so other kinds of technology must be used. For endangered mammals and birds, cloning may be a way of producing new animals. Cloning is when the genetic code of one individual is injected into an unfertilized egg whose own genetic code has been removed. In the U.S., a rare kind of wild sheep called a mouflon has been produced in this way. One method being experimented with now is cross-species cloning, where one species gives birth to the young of an endangered species. Some very rare kinds of fish might be saved by a new technique being developed in Japan. The Japanese researchers took young salmon and injected reproductive cells from an endangered fish species. The result was salmon that gave birth to fish of the endangered species.

Many people are opposed to cloning, and at present the technique is not good enough to be really useful in saving a whole species. However, some zoos are freezing small amounts of tissue from endangered animals, in the hope that in the future it will be possible to clone new animals from the tissue.

Although these types of technology may help save particular animals and plants, technology alone will not save species in the long run. To do this, we need to conserve the habitats where the plants and animals live.

Mouflon sheep like these were the first endangered wild animals to be cloned. Some scientists think this may be a way to save endangered species. Others think it is a false hope.

FOR AND AGAINST

For
- Cloning can increase the number of individuals if a population becomes extremely small.
- If we collect and save tissue samples before animal populations get too small, cloning could provide an "insurance policy" if a species almost disappears.
- Cloning may make it possible to bring back genetic material from animals that cannot breed.
- Any tool that might save endangered species is useful.

Against
- The science of cloning is still very untried. There are many problems with the process that still need solving.
- Many species have not yet been successfully cloned.
- Cloned individuals often have poor health and die earlier than normal.
- Cloning gives a false sense of security that populations of endangered animals can easily be revived.

Changing farming A lot of the food we eat is grown on large farms with fields full of one kind of crop, or in orchards and plantations containing only one kind of tree. Using this type of farming, we have managed to produce far more food from the land than we could in the past.

However, we are beginning to learn that this kind of farming has long-term problems. In some places it has destroyed the soil, leaving dusty desert areas. Modern farming methods can also cause pollution of the land and water. Farmers use fertilizers to improve the soil and pesticides to kill off insects and other pests. Putting all these chemicals on the land year after year can cause long-term damage. Also, some of the chemicals are washed away by the rain and pollute streams and rivers. The polluted water can harm wildlife.

One technology that might help farmers to avoid fertilizers and pesticides is genetic modification. Genetically modified (GM) plants are plants that have had genes from another plant or animal added to them. Food crops can be genetically modified to resist pests or diseases, so farmers do not need to use pesticides to protect them. However, many people do not see GM as environment-friendly technology.

One way of cutting down on the use of pesticides is to use GM plants that can resist pests, like these cotton plants in the U.S. However, some people strongly oppose the use of GM crops.

Another technique is to combine modern farming methods with techniques used in the past. Co-planting involves planting together pairs of crops that complement each other. For instance, if wheat is planted with red clover, the red clover keeps down weeds and adds nitrogen back

FOR AND AGAINST

For
- Plants can be genetically modified to resist pests and diseases. Farmers then have to use fewer pesticides and herbicides.
- Some GM plants can produce better yields than ordinary crops.

Against
- Many GM crops are not sustainable: farmers cannot use seeds from crops they grow and plant them the following year.
- Some GM crops are designed to be resistant to pesticides. Farmers use more pesticides on these types of crops, not less.
- GM crops can crossbreed with ordinary crops and "contaminate" them. This is a particular problem for organic crops, which are sold at high prices.
- GM plants could crossbreed with wild plants and create "superweeds."

to the soil. Scientists working in Canada have found that farmers can get good yields of crops using less herbicides and pesticides with techniques such as co-planting.

Acid rain Some of the chemicals released into the air by cars and factories contain sulfur or nitrogen. When it rains, some of these chemicals dissolve in the rain as it falls. They make the rain acid. The acid rain has its strongest effects on lakes and rivers, where it can be very harmful to fish and other water life.

The best way to stop acid rain is to stop releasing pollutants in smoke. Many new technologies have been developed to "scrub" the smoke from coal power stations and other factories producing the gases that cause acid rain. Filters and devices that use static electricity get rid of most of the soot and other particles from the smoke. Materials such as powdered limestone, seawater, and caustic soda are used in "wet scrubbers" to absorb sulfur gases from the smoke. Improving the way fuels are burned and recirculating gases through the furnace are methods used to get rid of nitrogen gases.

Scientists test the acidity of a frozen lake in Canada as part of research into the effects of acid rain.

WHAT'S NEXT?

Scientists are investigating various ways of stopping too much carbon dioxide from getting into the air by "capturing" the carbon dioxide before it escapes from factory chimneys and car exhausts. Trapping the carbon dioxide in this way is relatively easy. Once it has been captured, the carbon dioxide has to be stored, to stop it from getting back into the air. Some oil companies in Norway already store captured carbon dioxide by pumping it into old oil and gas fields under the North Sea. The carbon dioxide should remain buried in the rocks for millions of years.

CHAPTER 6
putting ideas together

Environmental technology is not just about saving energy, reusing waste, finding new kinds of fuel, or improving the natural environment. It is about doing many of these things at once, as part of an overall plan for sustainable, low-energy living. If things are planned well, different technologies work together, and the results are better than when we use each kind of technology by itself.

One place where careful planning has made a whole city "green" is in Curitiba in southern Brazil. Curitiba is famous around the world as an example of good environmental design. Each area of the city is designed as a unit, including houses, shops, and businesses close to each other, so that many people can walk or cycle to work. For people who have to travel farther, there is a very efficient, fast bus service, with buses arriving every 30 seconds at the busiest times. Two-thirds of the city's garbage is recycled. In the poorest areas, where garbage trucks cannot get to the houses, people can take their garbage to collection points and swap it for free travel tickets or food. The city has large numbers of green spaces, with thousands of trees planted by volunteers. Many public buildings are places that were recycled rather than newly built. For instance, an old glue factory was turned into a theater, and a warehouse became a community center. These kinds of

Curitiba's buses load very quickly because tickets are bought in advance and passengers can get on through several doors. Even the design of the bus shelters helps.

WHAT'S NEXT?

A city in the United Arab Emirates is planned to be the first in the world to be zero-carbon. It will use no fossil fuel energy, all waste will be recycled, and it will use 80 percent less water than a normal city. Masdar, as it is called, will be a research center for sustainable development where nearly 50,000 people will live. The streets will be narrow and shaded, and no private cars will be allowed. No one will live more than 1/8 mile (200 m) from a stopping place for an efficient electric personal transportation system. A large solar power plant will be built by 2009. The power from this plant will be used to build the rest of the city.

An artist's impression of how Masdar will look. The narrow streets and covered walkways will help keep the city streets cool in the hot climate.

conversions kept down the initial energy costs of the buildings. Despite having grown from a city of just 150,000 in the 1950s to 1.6 million people today, it is still a spacious, pleasant place to live.

Curitiba's sustainable planning began in the 1970s, well before other cities began to think about planning for a better environment. However, today other large cities are beginning to make their own sustainable plans. New York, for instance, has a 25-year plan, which will involve planting more than a million trees, cleaning up pollution in the rivers, and charging cars that want to go into the busiest parts of the city.

Planned from scratch One of the most exciting hopes for the future of the environment is the city of Dongtan, just outside Shanghai, China. Dongtan will be a city of 500,000 people, built on a swampy island in the mouth of the Yangtze River. Dongtan will have many lakes and canals, because it is built in a small area on one side of the island. Around the city will be parks, farmland, and a large area of untouched wetland for birds. It is planned that the first stage of the city will be built by 2010.

An architect discusses an artist's impression of what Dongtan will look like.

HOW IT WORKS

Here are some ideas planned for Dongtan.

Cars and buses will run with hydrogen or other renewable fuels. Solar-powered water taxis will travel along canals and lakes. Cycle paths and footpaths will make it easy to get around on foot or by bike. Most importantly, the city will be planned as a cluster of separate villages, so that everyone lives within walking distance of stores, schools, and workplaces.

An energy supply center will include a biofuel power station using rice hulls as fuel, wind turbines, and a power station using waste material.

Low-energy buildings will be made using local materials, high insulation, solar panels, and green roofs (roofs covered with earth and plants).

There will be two water networks, one for drinking water, one for toilet flushing and irrigating (watering) farmland. This second will be treated wastewater.

However, the new city will not just be a nice place to live: it will be a green city. At one edge, there will be a large power plant using biofuel made from rice hulls (the outside parts that are usually thrown away). Heat from the power plant will be used to warm the city's houses and apartments. There will also be a wind farm and a power plant fueled by the city's waste. As in Curitiba, the city is planned in small districts, so that people do not have to travel far to go to work or go shopping. The lake and canal system will not just be for show: it will also act as a reservoir for preventing floods. Buildings will naturally be low energy, with solar panels to supply even more of the city's energy. All of the city's energy will come from renewable sources, and two-thirds of the city's waste will be reused. If it works, Dongtan could be a blueprint for cities around the world.

Not the whole answer Saving the world from being damaged by global warming is a huge challenge for the human race. We have seen the many ways in which environmental technology can help by saving energy, reusing waste, finding new kinds of energy, and reducing pollution.

Technology alone will not save the world. People around the world will need to change their ideas of what is useful and valuable. When we buy a car, we need to value its energy efficiency more than how fast it goes. When we

Iceland may be the first country in the world to switch over from fossil fuels to hydrogen. Many buses and some cars in Iceland already run on hydrogen.

are looking for a new house, we need to check its insulation as well as the kitchen appliances. New technology will need to be coupled with new attitudes if we are hoping to save the Earth.

WHAT'S NEXT?

Iceland may be the first country to develop a hydrogen economy. The country has a plentiful supply of cheap electricity made by geothermal power (power from volcanic springs in the earth). This electricity is being used to make hydrogen from water. The first hydrogen filling station was opened in 2003, and a hydrogen-powered bus service began soon afterward. Next will come hydrogen-powered cars, then fishing boats. By 2050, the whole country could be running on hydrogen.

glossary

algae Plant-like living things. Most algae are microscopic, but seaweeds are also algae.

bacteria Microscopic living organisms that multiply by dividing. Some bacteria cause diseases.

bioethanol A biofuel made up mainly of ethanol, a kind of alcohol that comes from fermenting corn or grain.

biofuel Fuel made from plants or from animal waste.

biogas Gas produced by microbes digesting (breaking down) plant or animal waste.

carbon The element in graphite and diamonds; the most important element in living things.

crop rotation Growing different crops each year, as a way of keeping the soil healthy.

deciduous (tree) A tree whose leaves fall in autumn.

DNA Short for deoxyribonucleic acid, a molecule that contains the genetic instructions for how a living being lives and grows.

embodied energy The total amount of energy needed to make a material.

fossil fuels Coal, oil, and gas; fossil fuels are nonrenewable resources.

genes The way that living things pass on characteristics such as eye color from parent to child. Genes are pieces of a substance called DNA that carries all hereditary information.

global warming The gradual warming of the Earth's climate.

greenhouse gas A gas that causes global warming if it is released into the atmosphere.

hemp A plant grown for its fibers, which are used for rope, cloth, and in some kinds of building materials.

landfill A way of disposing of garbage by burying it.

methanol Also known as methyl alcohol: a colorless liquid that is used as a solvent, as a fuel, and as antifreeze in engines.

passive design Design of a house so that it gets energy passively from the environment, for example, from the sun.

photovoltaic cell (solar cell) A panel of semiconductor material that turns light energy into electricity.

sustainable Something that is sustainable can carry on indefinitely.

wind turbine A large propeller designed to turn in the wind.

Fashion
FORWARD

All Dolled Up

*Bringing 1920s and 1930s
Flair to Your Wardrobe*

by Rebecca Langston-George

Consultant:
Hazel Clark, PhD
Research Chair of Fashion
Parsons The New School for Design
New York, New York

Savvy Books are published by Capstone Press,
1710 Roe Crest Drive, North Mankato, Minnesota 56003
www.capstonepub.com

Library of Congress Cataloging-in-Publication Data
Langston-George, Rebecca.
All dolled up : bringing 1920s and 1930s flair to your wardrobe / by Rebecca Langston-George.
pages cm.—(Savvy. Fashion forward)
Includes bibliographical references and index.
Summary: "Describes the fashion trends of the 1920s and 1930s, including step-by-step instructions
on how to get the looks today"—Provided by publisher.
Audience: Age 10-14.
Audience: Grade 4 to 6.
ISBN 978-1-4765-3997-3 (library binding) — ISBN 978-1-4765-6158-5 (ebook pdf)
1. Dress accessories—Juvenile literature. 2. Clothing and dress—United States—History—
20th century—Juvenile literature. I. Title.
TT649.8.L56 2014
646'.3—dc23   2013023076

Editorial Credits
Jennifer Besel, editor; Tracy Davies McCabe, designer; Marcie Spence, media researcher;
    Jennifer Walker, production specialist

Photo Credits
Alamy Images: Everett Collection, Inc., 20 (right), 46, Images.com, 4; Art Resource, N.Y.: The Metropolitan
Museum of Art, 52 (bottom); Bridgeman Art Library: Philadelphia Museum of Art, 54; Capstone Studio:
Karon Dubke, 5, 9 (bottom), 11, 13, 17 (headband), 21 (shoes), 27, 29, 36, 37, 43, 51, 53, 55, 59; Corbis:
Bettmann, 8 (left), Conde Nast Archive, 24; Getty Images: Alinari Archives, Florence, 18, Central Press,
48 (left), Chicago History Musuem, 7, Clarence Sinclair Bull/FPG/Archive Photos, 38 (left), Donato
Sardellia/WireImage, 28 (middle), FPG/Hulton Archive, 14, General Photographic Agency, 31 (top left),
Hulton Archive, 12 (top), 25 (bottom), Imagno, 23, 44 (left), James Devaney/WireImage, 28 (right), 35,
Jean Baptiste LaCroix/WireImage, 58 (right), Jef Kravitz/FilmMagic, 57 (left), Jesse Grant/WireImages, 19
(left), John Kobal Foundation, 42 (left), Michael Buckner/WireImage, 58 (left), Popperfoto/Bob Thomas,
20 (left), Ron Galella Collection, 25 (top left), Sasha, 26 (top), 30, Tim Graham, 25 (top middle), Time Life
Pictures/Mansell, 32 (left); House of Francheska, 50; iStockphoto: eliferen, 33 (hat); Library of Congress: 22
(bottom), 39; Newscom: Solo/ZUMA Press, 56 (left); Shutterstock: Africa Studio, 49 (jacket), Alan Poulson
Photography, 33 (socks), angelo gilardelli, 15 (top), Anna Tyukhmeneva, design element, anneka, 16, Azuzl,
design element, caimacanul, 49 (tie), catwalker, 56 (right), Dana E. Fry, cover, Eky Studio, design element,
El Greco, 21 (scarf), Eleonora Kolomiyets, design element, Everett Collection, 28 (left), 31 (bottom middle
and middle right), 34, Featureflash, 12 (bottom), 15 (bottom left), 32 (right), 42 (right), 44 (right), 57 (right),
60 (middle and right), 61 (right), FrameAngel, 17 (bag), Gordana Sermek, (sweater), 33 (shirt), grynold, 31
(middle left), Hakan Kizitan, 31 (bottom left), happykanppy, design element, Hector Sanchez, 19 (middle),
Helga Esteb, 8 (right), 25 (top right), Jaguar PS, 52 (top), Joe Seer, 15 (bottom right), 41, 61 (left), Karkas,
17 (skirt), 21 (skirt), 31 (top middle), Kellis, cover (pearls), L.F., 31 (top right), Lena Ivanova, 33 (pants),
Lisovskaya Natalia, 17 (pearls), Marilyn Volan, design element, maxstockphoto, 31 (middle), Medvedka,
design element, Natalia Matveeva, 31 (bottom right), Natykach Natalia, design element, Nejron Photo, 40,
Oksancia, design element, Olena Zaskochenko, cover, 9 (top left), Olga Ekaterincheva, 45, pashabo, design
element, Photo Works, 15 (bottom middle), Pietus, design element, Rene Schild, 22 (top), Richard Peterson,
21 (hat), s_bukley, 38 (right), 47, 48 (right), sagir, 21 (shirt), 49 (pants), 60 (left), Sharon Alexander, 19 (right),
spillman, 49 (hat), Stargazer, design element, worldswildlifewonders, 26 (bottom)

Printed in the United States of America in Brainerd, Minnesota.
092013   007770BANGS14

Table of Contents

WHAT'S OLD IS NEW

Take a look inside your closet. The clothes there reflect your personality, taste, and style. They also reflect the trends of today. But look closer. You likely have separate pieces that you pair together, such as sweaters and skirts. You probably have a T-shirt with a funny picture or saying on it. Maybe you have makeup and headbands on your dresser. All those styles and accessories aren't modern inventions. You'll have to go all the way back to the 1920s and 1930s to find the inspiration for many styles you wear today.

Women's clothing underwent a revolution in the '20s and '30s. For the first time in history, women showed their legs and bare arms. They began to imitate the styles of movie stars and sports figures. And women's clothing got freer!

The styles of these decades left a lasting impression on fashion. Everyone recognizes the fringed, low-waisted flapper dresses of the '20s. The poised look of the 1930s' high-waisted sailor pant is still worn today. You can't deny that the looks are timeless. And that's why we still love to wear them.

You can bring even more of these iconic styles into your look. With a little bling and some style know-how, you can become a '20s and '30s fashionista. Retro fashion is new fashion!

RETRO
FASHION
IS NEW
FASHION

GOOD-BYE CORSETS, HELLO LEGS!

The Roaring Twenties were a time of wild excess. The music was loud, and the dances were shocking. Young women wore shorter dresses and hairstyles than ever before. Some people called the fashions scandalous.

Wild dances such as the Charleston swept across the United States. These new dances required clothes that allowed dancers' arms and legs to move freely. If you had to sum up 1920s style in one word, it would be legs. Hems rose as high as the knees for the first time in modern history. Short dresses even replaced long dresses for fancy evening wear. Legs that had long been covered by full skirts were now everywhere.

Major law changes during this decade gave people both freedom and restriction. In August 1920 Congress passed the 19th Amendment, granting women the right to vote. This new freedom was a sign of the changing times. Women wouldn't be held back any longer. The loose, relaxed styles were just one outward sign of this new attitude.

In January 1920, the 18th Amendment banned alcohol. Prohibition had a deep effect on life in the 1920s. Men and women went to secret speakeasies to party. The popularity of this underground scene led to the rebellious, free-spirited attitude the 1920s is remembered for.

Fabulous Flappers

The daring flapper has been revived today.

No group was more rebellious or free-spirited than the young women called flappers. Flappers were liberal women who drove cars and danced the nights away. They came to symbolize the attitudes of the 1920s.

Flappers wore dresses decorated with rows of fringe or glass beads that swayed in rhythm to their dance moves. No tight waists or corsets for these girls! Instead, they wore boxy shaped dresses with loose, dropped waists. Bare arms swung to the beat of the music.

The daring flapper has been revived today. Katy Perry and Carrie Underwood have both been spotted in flapper inspired clothing.

In June 2012 Perry wore a flapper headband and long pearls. Her peach floor-length evening gown added to the vintage look.

Flapper styles are popular on dance floors too. Celebs on *Dancing with the Stars* often wear beaded outfits that sway with their fancy footwork.

Movies have brought back the carefree and fresh styles of the '20s too. The 2013 movie *The Great Gatsby* showcased fringed flappers. The successful movie had people roaring for the looks themselves. Brands such as Fogal and Brooks Brothers released new lines inspired by the movie. And countless blogs and news shows told viewers how to get the looks for less.

Get the *Look*

Long strands of beads that swung around while dancing where very popular in the 1920s. A single extra-long strand of beads might be hard to find now. But you can make your own from two shorter strands.

SUPPLIES

- 2 matching strands of beads

1. Lay the two strands end to end on your workspace, overlapping slightly.
2. Where the strands overlap, pull the bottom strand up over the top one to make a circle.
3. Bring the bottom of the strand nearest you up to the circle. Pull it under the circle you just made.
4. Pull until the strand goes all the way through to knot the strands together.

Get the *Look*

Change a plain summer dress into a flapper sensation. Check your closet or hit the thrift store for a knee-length tank dress. Then add some fringe for a flapper makeover.

SUPPLIES

- sewing measuring tape
- solid-colored knee-length tank dress
- scissors
- 2-inch (5-centimeter) long chainette fringe in a complimentary color to your dress
- pins
- thread to match the fringe
- needle

1. Measure around the bottom of the dress.
2. Add 1 inch (2.5 cm) to your measurement.
3. Cut three pieces of fringe the length you calculated in step 2.
4. Pin one piece of fringe around the bottom of the dress. The ends should overlap in the back, and the fringe should hang below the hem line.
5. Sew the fringe in place, starting in the back and working your way around the dress. When you get back to the end, fold the last ½-inch (1-cm) of fringe under itself and stitch it in place.
6. Pin another row of fringe above the first so they overlap slightly. Sew that row in place.
7. Repeat step 6 to make a third row of fringe. Now you're ready for the dance floor!

1920s
Hair and Makeup

Just like today's young women, flappers imitated the hairstyles and makeup of popular actresses. Celebs in those days were silent movie stars. Actress Louise Brooks' short bobbed hair was all the rage. Women raced to beauty salons to shake out their hairpins and cut their long hair.

If you think the bobbed hair of the 1920s is out, think again. Take a look at the bob Katie Holmes wore. The inspiration is unmistakable.

Get the Look

Headbands and combs with colorful feathers were popular 1920s accessories. No matter what length you wear your hair, you can jazz up your locks flapper style.

SUPPLIES

- hot glue gun and glue
- two small, colorful feathers
- fancy button with a shank
- ½-inch (1-cm) wide or wider elastic headband
- marker
- needle and thread

1. Hot glue the feathers to the back of the button.
2. Put the headband on. It should go over your hair and across your forehead.
3. While looking in a mirror, make a small dot on the headband where you want the feathers and button to go. They should be off to one side, between your eye and ear.
4. Take off the headband. Sew the button to the headband on the dot you made in step 3.
5. Wear the headband across your forehead flapper style.

ovie stars also introduced women to makeup, which most young women of the time had never worn. Silent actress Clara Bow was famous for her lipstick pout, much like Angelina Jolie is known for her full lips today. Bow's look made young women line up to buy lipstick for the first time. Their parents were horrified!

CLARA BOW

Get the Look

Silent movie stars made a powerful statement without talking. But their bold pouty lips sure spoke to the audience. To get Clara's perfect pout, all you need is a tube of bright red lipstick. There was no lip liner, gloss, or stain back then. Stand in front of the mirror and pucker up. Apply the lipstick heavily to the middle of your lips. Narrow the line of lipstick as you reach the corners of the lips.

Today's celebs continue the pouty tradition. You're sure to see it on the red carpet and in magazines. Scarlett Johansson, Drew Barrymore, and Taylor Swift have all pulled off the pout.

PUT IT
TOGETHER

Put together a flapper inspired look with modern pieces.

Party and costume stores often carry 1920s headbands. But you can easily make your own too.

Check accessory shops for long necklaces and flashy beaded bags. Don't forget to check the attic too. You never know what your great-grandma might have saved for you.

Department stores will have sequined tank tops that show off that fun flare. Pair a tank with a knee-length pencil skirt for this '20s inspired outfit.

A quick online search for "Mary Jane shoes" will bring up hundreds of options. Have fun choosing the right pair for you!

Everyday *Elegance*

The beads and fringe of flapper dresses were perfect for the dance floor. But they weren't very practical for daily life. Women needed comfortable, stylish clothing for everyday wear. One designer who understood this need was Coco Chanel.

Around the beginning of World War I (1914–1918), Chanel began designing clothes using a light knit fabric called jersey. Until then jersey had only been used to make men's underwear. But Chanel liked the soft, stretchy fabric and thought women would find it comfortable. She created women's separates. Chanel's separates, unlike dresses, were outfits made up of individual pieces. Skirts, blouses, and sweaters that can be mixed and matched are called sportswear separates. Much like the loose, flowing flapper dresses, these pieces were unfitted and sporty. The popularity of this fashion proved that the 1920s woman wanted to be both fashionable and able to move.

Today's women still want to be fashionable and comfortable. Everybody, even A-list celebs, still wear sportswear fashions. Nicole Richie's Winter Kate collection even includes throwback fashions inspired by the 1920s' sportswear trend.

COCO CHANEL

Scent-sational

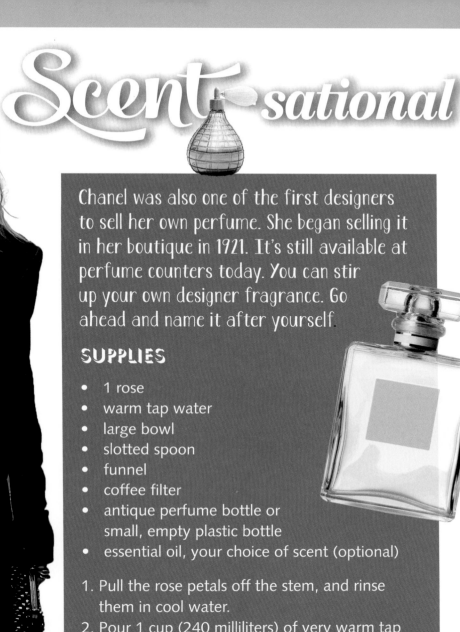

Chanel was also one of the first designers to sell her own perfume. She began selling it in her boutique in 1921. It's still available at perfume counters today. You can stir up your own designer fragrance. Go ahead and name it after yourself.

SUPPLIES

- 1 rose
- warm tap water
- large bowl
- slotted spoon
- funnel
- coffee filter
- antique perfume bottle or small, empty plastic bottle
- essential oil, your choice of scent (optional)

1. Pull the rose petals off the stem, and rinse them in cool water.
2. Pour 1 cup (240 milliliters) of very warm tap water into a bowl.
3. Push the petals into the water. Let them sit overnight.
4. In the morning remove the petals from the water with a slotted spoon.
5. If you wish, add up to 10 drops of essential oil to the rose water. Stir gently.
6. Line a funnel with a coffee filter. Strain the rose water into the perfume bottle. Use the perfume within a few days.

NICOLE RICHIE

THE GATSBY LOOK

Designer Jean Patou took Chanel's sporty separates to another level—actual sports! In 1921 he created a tennis outfit for French player Suzanne Lenglen. She wore a knee-length pleated white skirt and sleeveless white cardigan. It made a huge sensation. Lenglen could move like today's tennis stars in her new clothing. And she looked fabulous doing it.

Everyday fashions began to copy Lenglen's look. Today this sporty style is called the Great Gatsby look. The term comes from F. Scott Fitzgerald's 1925 novel *The Great Gatsby*. Stars such as Blake Lively keep the pleated skirt fashionable. Separates that can be mixed and matched are the staples of today's wardrobe. The separates in your closet have a lot in common with the sporty trend of the 1920s.

Today this sporty style is often called the Great Gatsby look.

SUZANNE LENGLEN

BLAKE LIVELY

PUT IT TOGETHER

Pair these modern pieces together, and show off your own Gatsby look.

Grab a plain white T-shirt from your closet.

Look for a sporty pleated skirt in a local store's sportswear department.

Find a long solid-color cardigan from a neighborhood thrift shop.

Tie on some cute white canvas tennis shoes. Sometimes you can even find these at a dollar store.

Dig through your grandma's closet to find a vintage cloche hat. Accessory stores carry these too.

Grab a long, knit white or striped scarf to finish off the look.

Athletic Clothing

The popularity of Lenglen's tennis outfit inspired new trends. Patou and other designers made clothes for other sports. Finally female athletes had clothing that they could play in. No more long, full skirts and big hats. Women could buy golf outfits, ski outfits, and stylish bathing suits in addition to tennis wear. The public's opinion of the outdoors changed with the styles.

In earlier times women stayed out of the sun. They wore large brimmed hats and gloves to cover up. Suddenly sunshine and outdoor sports became stylish.

Of course, athletic clothing is a booming business even today. Tennis star Venus Williams' clothing line EleVen features trendy clothes for active women. Yesterday's sports clothes definitely paved the way for today's gym clothes and yoga pants.

Wearing Pants

Women almost never wore pants before the late 1920s. But the carefree '20s changed that too. Women's pants started as casual wear for the wealthy. Swimsuit coverings called bathing pajamas became popular. They were followed by lounging pajamas. These pajamas weren't meant for sleep. However, women didn't wear them in public. Lounging pajamas were flowing, comfortable items to wear around the house. Wearing pants outside the house would start to take off in the 1930s.

LOUNGING PAJAMAS

The Little Black Dress

Chanel also popularized the black dress fashion trend that remains a must-have to this day. The "Little Black Dress," or LBD, became a hit in the 1920s. Chanel's LBDs were fashionable, yet simple. The dresses could go from afternoon to evening wear with the simple switch of a hat. Women loved them!

Chanel's first LBD design had long sleeves and was made of wool, velvet, or satin. But the dress soon came in many variations, including short sleeves and sleeveless and could be made with chiffon or lace.

The LBD trend is a long-lasting one. In fact, fashion gurus today still say that no wardrobe is complete without one. And like all trends, celebrities are on the front lines.

MOLLY RINGWALD 1987

PRINCESS DIANA 1995

HALLE BERRY 2012

AUDREY HEPBURN
1961

ACCESSORIZING

Just like today, the modern 1920s woman enjoyed accessorizing with scarves, hats, and costume jewelry. A scarf was essential for the Gatsby look. The perfect scarf for the sporty look was long and narrow. It was typically knitted and often fringed at the bottom. Plain white scarves or horizontally striped ones were popular.

But how a woman wore it was just as important as which scarf she chose. The scarf was wrapped around the neck once. One end was worn down the front and the other down the back.

In the 2010s scarves came roaring back as a fashion craze. Today's scarves come in all kinds of styles and are tied in hundreds of ways. But it's fun to see the 1920s scarf trend revived in a new way.

KELLY ROWLAND
SINGER

Get the Look

Make your own Gatsby scarf. No-sew blanket fleece from the fabric store is perfect for this project.

SUPPLIES:

- white fleece, 7 inches (18 cm) wide by 58 inches (147 cm) long
- ruler
- pencil
- scissors
- tape

1. Lay the fleece across your workspace so one short end faces you.
2. Measure 2½ inches (6 cm) up from the end, and make a light pencil mark on the fleece.
3. Lay a piece of tape across the width of the fabric at the mark you made in step 2.
4. Measure ¼ inch (.6 cm) from the left side below the tape line. Make a light pencil mark. Continue measuring across the width of the fleece, making marks at ¼-inch (.6-cm) intervals.
5. Create fringe by cutting the fleece from the bottom edge up to the tape, following the marks made in step 4. Remove the tape.
6. Repeat steps 2 through 5 on the other end of the fleece.

Costume jewelry was another popular accessory of the 1920s. Always the trend setter, Chanel sold costume jewelry as well as clothing. Inexpensive jewelry was not entirely new. It had been around since the 1800s. But it served a different purpose. Costume jewelry before the '20s was made to imitate real gems that a woman already owned. A woman might wear the cheaper copy while keeping her "real" jewelry locked in the safe.

Chanel made costume jewelry fashionable for everyone. Glass pearls and imitation gold were her signature pieces. In her words, "A girl should be two things: classy and fabulous." If you like looking fabulous, but don't want to break the bank, you can thank Chanel for affordable jewelry.

Hats really topped off the sporty outfits of the day. The hat style that ruled the 1920s was the cloche. A cloche fit snugly over the forehead. Covering the back of the neck and the ears, it was decorated with ribbons, beads, or feathers. Its popularity might be due to how well it fit over a bobbed haircut. Bobbed hair and cloche hats were made for each other.

Like scarves, cloche hats aren't hard to find these days. Model Marisa Miller wore one to the 2011 Kentucky Derby. Kelly Osbourne and Sarah Jessica Parker have been caught wearing these stunning 1920s hats too.

A GIRL SHOULD BE TWO THINGS: CLASSY AND FABULOUS

CRISTA B. ALLEN
ACTRESS

LEIGHTON MEESTER
ACTRESS

Get the Look

Add some decoration to a modern cloche hat to get that 1920s flair.

SUPPLIES

- leaf-shaped cookie cutter
- 3 sheets of felt, in complimentary colors to your hat
- pencil or marker
- scissors
- needle and thread
- colorful flat button
- hot glue gun and glue
- cloche hat, often found in the fall or winter at accessory stores

1. Lay the cookie cutter on a piece of felt. Trace around the cutter. Trace three leaves on each sheet of felt.
2. Cut out the felt leaves.
3. Arrange the leaves in a flower shaped pile, so you can see each one. Place the button in the center.
4. Sew the flower together through the button holes.
5. Hot glue the flower to one side of the hat.

Fancy *Footwork*

Today's shoes also share similarities with the shoes your great-grandmothers wore. Look for shoes with rounded edges, closed toes, and medium-high chunky heels. Mary Jane shoes with a strap across the front will give you a vintage look. So will T-straps, which have a vertical strap in addition to the Mary Jane strap.

Another modern shoe style that gets its look from the '20s is the shootie. Shootie is a combination of the word shoe and boot. Modern shooties come up the foot all the way to the ankle. Vintage ones aren't quite as tall. But they all give a fantastic flapper feel.

SLIMMER CLOTHES FOR SLIMMER TIMES

The good times of the Roaring Twenties came to a sudden halt in October 1929. The stock market crashed, and the world plummeted into the Great Depression (1929–1939). Many people lost their jobs and their homes. No one felt like dancing anymore. And no one had extra cash for fancy clothes. The feathers, fringe, and beads of the carefree flapper days went out of style.

As the nation's mood fell so did dress hems. Knee-length dresses and skirts were replaced by hems that fell to mid-calf. The importance of legs in the last decade changed to an interest in feminine curves. Boxy, dropped waist dresses were out. They were replaced by more fitted clothing that hugged the waist.

Belted dresses showed off a slim waist. Separates also became more closely fitted to the body. The long, loose cardigans of the '20s turned into shorter, shapelier sweaters and jackets.

These trends didn't die out when the economy improved. Belted dresses and short jackets are still everywhere. Michelle Obama rocks the belted, longer hem look. Nicki Minaj and Catherine, Duchess of Cambridge have worn '30s inspired jackets.

CATHERINE
DUCHESS OF CAMBRIDGE

PUT IT TOGETHER

During the Great Depression, people got the latest news by purchasing newspapers from boys on the street. The 1930s newsboy look is easy to re-create.

Modern newsboy caps are popular. You can find them at just about any accessory or department store.

Raid your brother's or dad's closets for a plain white T-shirt.

Find some colorful suspenders to complement your socks. Grandpa's closet or a thrift store would be great places to look for these.

A pair of khakis that you already have will work fine. Just roll them up to mid-calf.

A funky pair of knee-high socks are the key to this look.

Popular  Pants

Practical and comfortable, pants became common casual wear by the mid-1930s. The most popular style was the sailor pant. These wide-legged, high-waisted pants didn't have zippers. Instead they were fastened with two rows of buttons at the front. The 1930s woman completed the look with sweaters.

Even this retro fashion is still very much in style. Christina Aguilera and Gwen Stefani made waves sporting sailor pants. The Ralph Lauren brand sells several wide-leg, high-waisted pants too.

CHRISTINA AGUILERA

Bare No More

The bare arms of the flapper days left with the 1920s. The conservative sleeves of the '30s came in many styles. Many of the same sleeve types hanging in your closet today were popular then. Long sleeves came plain, cuffed, or banded at the wrist. Short sleeves might have bows, cuffs, or lace in a contrasting color. The loose, fluttering sleeve that falls just below the shoulder was popular too.

Get the Look

Give an old T-shirt new life with a retro 1930s look.

SUPPLIES

- long sleeve solid color T-shirt
- ruler
- piece of chalk
- scissors
- needle
- thread
- pins

1. Turn the shirt inside out. Lay it flat, and smooth out any wrinkles. Make sure the seams are lined up.
2. Lay the ruler at the top of one sleeve where it meets the shoulder. Measure down the sleeve. Make a chalk mark at 5 inches (13 cm) and 10 inches (25 cm).

3. Chalk a line from the armpit seam to the 10-inch (25-cm) mark. Cut along this line to remove the sleeve. Set the cut off sleeve aside.

4. Chalk a line from the top end of the now shortened sleeve up to the 5-inch (13-cm) mark. Cut a slit up to the 5-inch mark.

5. Tie the two sides of the slit together in a double knot. Voila! You now have a short bow-tie sleeve.

6. Repeat steps 1–5 on the other sleeve. Then turn the shirt right-side out.

7. Grab one of the cut off sleeves. Lay it flat and smooth out any wrinkles. Cut off the hem and the side seam.

8. Cut two long strips from the sleeve. They should be as long as the sleeve and 2 inches (5 cm) wide.

9. Place one strip on top of the other. Sew a seam along one of the 2-inch (5-cm) ends.

10. Open the strips up into one long strip. Press the seam open with an iron.

11. Lay the strip horizontally on your work space. Starting with the long top edge, roll the strip into a burrito. Pin the middle of the fabric roll to the middle of the T-shirt's neck.

12. Sew the fabric roll to the T-shirt with a few stitches.

13. Tie the fabric roll into a bow.

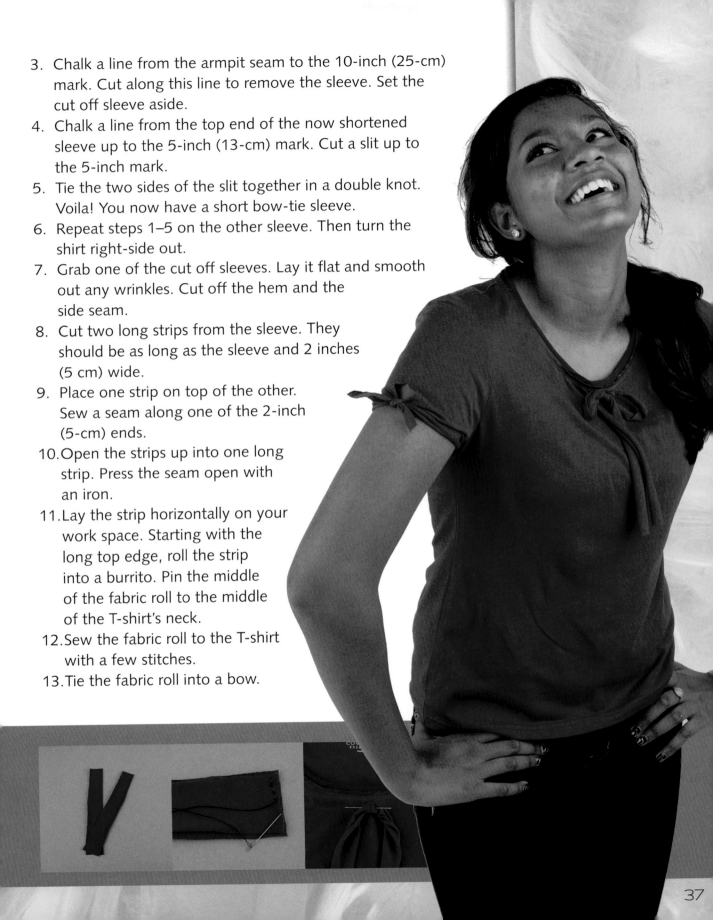

Bibs and Bows

Even though they didn't have much money, women in the 1930s wanted to look good. You know that feeling, right? Adding ruffles, bibs, and bows to plain dresses became a cheap, easy way for women to spruce up their wardrobes. One Sears catalog in 1935 showed 15 styles of detachable collars women could purchase for as little as 39 cents.

Sleeves and necklines drew attention up to women's faces. Interesting sleeves and necklines also added volume to the top of the body, creating a curvier look. The collar necklace trend today is a throwback to the 1930s. Elizabeth Banks, Vanessa Hudgens, Kristen Stewart, and Victoria Justice, are just a few of the celebs going for this retro look.

> The collar necklace trend today is a throwback to the 1930s.

VIRGINIA BRUCE ACTRESS

ELIZABETH BANKS ACTRESS

Plates and Snoods

Collars weren't the only accessory that came in many styles. Hat makers had fewer materials to make hats during the Depression. So the brimmed cloche fell out of favor. Instead smaller, more open hats, called button plate hats took center stage. These hats were worn at an angle near the back of the head. They were kept in place with hat pins. Some were trimmed with bows, small flowers, or pins.

The snood is possibly one of the most well-known 1930s accessories. A snood was a crocheted or knitted net that kept the hair back. Snoods were an easy accessory to make at home. With little money for shopping, 1930s women made do-it-yourself hats popular fashion.

Making Waves

Hems and sleeves weren't the only fashions that dropped during the Great Depression. In the 1930s women let their bobbed hair grow longer. Soft, wavy hairdos replaced straight, slick bobs. A style called finger waves became the hair sensation of the decade. Finger waves were S-shaped curves that zigzagged down the side of the face. Some women got their hair set in permanent waves at the beauty parlor. But to save money, many women set their hair in finger waves at home.

Beautiful hair never goes out of style. Finger waves are a classic. You'll often see modern versions of these waves on the red carpet. Taylor Swift regularly wears finger waves in her hair. She's even picked up a few Grammy awards sporting the look. Model Tyra Banks also likes to experiment with this look.

Get the Look

Finger waves are a tricky look to create at first. But after some practice, you'll have the sleek, retro look that will make heads turn.

SUPPLIES

- a fine-toothed comb
- hair gel
- several long duckbill or alligator hair clips
- curlers

1. Start with clean, damp (but not wet) hair. Use a comb to make a clean side part.
2. Comb a generous amount of gel through the hair on the left side of the part.
3. Press your right pointer finger firmly along the part. The finger should point toward your forehead.
4. Lay your middle finger on your hair. Pinch up the hair between your pointer and middle fingers to create a little wave. Press your fingers down firmly on your head to hold the hair in place.
5. As you hold down the hair, use your other hand to gently comb the hair below the pinched wave toward the back of your head.
6. Put the comb down and place clips where your fingers were holding down the hair. The clips should point toward your forehead.
7. Press your pointer finger firmly on your head just below the lowest clip. Repeat steps 4–6 to create another wave. This time comb the hair below the wave toward your face, and point the clips toward the back of your head.
8. Continue making waves down the side of your head, alternating the direction of the combing and clips.
9. Repeat steps 2–8 on the other side of your head.
10. Comb gel through the hair left in the back. Roll it in curlers.
11. Let your hair dry completely with the clips and curlers in place. Then remove the clips and curlers. Use your fingers to brush through the back of your hair.

GOLDEN AGE OF STYLE

Real life during the Great Depression was difficult. But life on the big screen was adventurous. A movie ticket cost just a quarter in the mid-1930s. It was a cheap way to forget your troubles for a couple of hours. The public packed theaters to watch their favorite stars. Movie tickets today cost more than a quarter, but they're still popular entertainment. And movie stars still rule the world of glamorous fashion.

Red carpet fashions date back to the first Academy Awards. It was held at the Hollywood Roosevelt Hotel in 1929. Stars wore long, elegant evening gowns. Floor-length gowns that hugged the body were the style. Legs were covered but backs were daringly bare. Watch any red carpet event, and you can see this is a trend that continues today.

RIHANNA

BETTE DAVIS

Get the Look

You don't have to wait for a red carpet invitation to try the bare-back look. Keep it young and modern by updating the back of a T-shirt.

SUPPLIES

- a piece of paper
- scissors
- a T-shirt in your choice of color and style
- pins
- chalk
- seam sealant for fabric
- hot glue gun and glue
- gemstones

1. Fold the piece of paper in half. Cut out half of a fat heart shape. Unfold the heart.
2. Turn the shirt inside out. Pin the heart on the upper back side of the shirt.
3. Trace a chalk line around the heart. Remove the paper pattern.
4. Cut along the line to make a heart that gives a peek at your back.
5. Turn the shirt right side out. Use seam sealant around the cut edges of the heart using package directions.
6. Hot glue gemstones around the heart to give it a finished look.

A Little Bias

Hollywood's 1930s glam styles were a stark contrast to the dim real world. Parisian designer Madeleine Vionnet played a huge role in those stunning styles. She created dresses by cutting fabric at an angle across its weave. This method, called the bias cut, allowed fabric to drape and follow a body's curves.

While bias cutting might not sound very exciting, the effect it had on fashion and society was shocking. Dresses in the 1930s began to cling tightly to bare skin. Every natural curve of the body was displayed. Garments no longer hid the female form—they celebrated it.

The glamorous starlet look is still around today. Look for long, simple shapes that hug the body. The focus is on the cut and drape of the dress. These gowns are often a solid color. Bare backs are another clue to a vintage look.

Some of the stars who have been spotted looking like they walked off the 1930s red carpet include Charlize Theron, Kate Winslet, and Jessica Chastain. Angelina Jolie's gown for the 2012 Golden Globes is an example of a modern starlet look. It was a draped blush-colored gown with a red triangle at the neckline.

The glamorous starlet look is still around today.

PENNY SINGLETON

ANGELINA JOLIE

Get the *Look*

Women of the '30s wore makeup more frequently than their 1920s sisters. In addition to lipstick, mascara and eye shadow were added. Pink tones were all the rage.

To get the look, dab pink cream blush on your cheeks along the cheekbones. Add a shimmery pink eye shadow over the top of the eyelid. Apply mascara to the top eyelashes only. Finish with loose powder from a powder puff. Finally, give your lips a thin coat of raspberry colored lipstick.

Everyday *Glam*

2^{98}

Sears Present America's

MOST THRILLING FASHIONS DIRECT FROM NEW YORK

Unequaled in Smartness, Quality and Value!

All America comes to New York for Fashions. No other city has such great style authorities! Such facilities for gathering style information! That is why Sears built their own great Fashion Headquarters right in the heart of the style section of New York. Our buyers are constantly in the market! With them— at their elbow, consulting, selecting—is America's favorite stylist, Anne Williams. Read what she has to say in this catalog . . . listen to her style talks over the radio! She sees to it that every *right* style is offered you.

HOW TO ORDER FASHIONS

You can order from our nearest Mail Order House with other goods, or you can mail order for items listed, "Sent from New York," direct to Sears, Roebuck and Co., New York City. In either case, you pay the postage only from our nearest Mail Order House—and we rush delivery direct from New York to you.

AUTOGRAPHED FASHION
Worn in Hollywood by
Ginger Rogers

Beruffled— Yet Divinely SLENDER

YOU KNOW THE KIND OF entrancing "Pencil-Slim" figure Ginger Rogers has! All slim soft curves! Well, here is a dress as exciting and vivacious as Ginger herself! Beruffled at the shoulders, slim and slinky about the hips, a swirling flare at your feet! *The very newest silhouette* —That's why I selected it for you. It's Cotton Chiffon Seersucker, as light as silk, and cool and airy enough for the hottest July night. The back dips to a deep V, flowers blossom at your

Ginger Rogers

Year: 1935 S

I had you all in mind while selecting this wonderful fashion line. I included not only styles as worn by the slender movie stars, but styles for the stout, the short, the tall and the youngsters, too. I am for all of you!

During the Great Depression few women needed red carpet dresses. But they wanted clothes like the ones worn by stars on the big screen.

Hollywood styles were copied and sold in catalogs and stores. Stars such as Ginger Rogers and Loretta Young modeled the clothing featured in catalogs. For just $2.98 women could buy a bias cut dress. Catalogs also offered women "autographed fashion." These pieces had labels sewn in them that said, "An Autographed Fashion. Worn in Hollywood by ..." The name of the actress who wore the fashion was printed on the label. Department stores opened cinema shops. Women could buy copies of stars' garments there too.

Modern starlets don't just pose for the camera. Some, like Jennifer Hudson, Mary-Kate and Ashley Olsen, and Kim Kardashian, have cast themselves in new roles. They also have their own fashion lines. Just like the women in the 1930s, many of today's shoppers want their clothes signed by a star. Now that signature may prove your favorite star

MARY-KATE AND ASHLEY OLSEN

IT SUITS YOU

MARLENE DIETRICH

It was a new kind of rebellion.

ELLEN DEGENERES

*a*nother Hollywood look to emerge during this time was the masculine look. With the popularity of pants, some stars took to dressing in men's wear. Marlene Dietrich wore this look on and off screen. It became her signature look. This controversial style blurred the lines between men's and women's clothing. It was a new kind of rebellion.

The masculine look for female stars is still popular today. Kirsten Dunst, Penelope Cruz, and Rihanna are just a few celebs who have rocked the suit look. Mary-Kate and Ashley Olsen's fashion line Elizabeth and James makes trendy suits for the female body. But Ellen DeGeneres and Diane Keaton are probably the most famous names pulling off this look today.

PUT IT TOGETHER

Looking like a movie star doesn't mean you have to strut around in a floor-length evening gown. You can wear Marlene Dietrich's famous masculine look anywhere.

Top off your look with a funky fedora from the accessory store.

Borrow a white button-down collared shirt from your mom.

Raid your dad's closet for a fun tie to add a splash of color.

Find a pair of dress pants and a matching blazer at the thrift store.

REALLY UNREAL FASHIONS

Everyone from tennis stars to actresses influenced fashion design in the 1920s and 1930s. So it's no surprise that artists were interested in fashion too.

In the mid-1930s painters such as Salvador Dali were creating art in a new style called surrealism. Surreal art was often inspired by dreams. The pictures contained unusual things. Sometimes shocking or funny, the art was always unique. Dali called his art "hand-painted dream photographs."

Dali brought this style to fashion runways by working with clothing designer Elsa Schiaparelli. Together they made humorous clothing, jewelry, and accessories. One of Dali's most famous jewelry pieces for Schiaparelli was a brooch. The brooch looked like a pair of red rhinestone covered lips around a row of pearl teeth.

Get the *Look*

Make your own copy of
Dali's famous lips brooch.

SUPPLIES

- pencil
- white poster board
- scissors
- adhesive red gemstone strips
- adhesive pearl strip
- hot glue gun and glue
- flat back pin

1. Draw the shape of a pair of lips onto the poster board. The drawing should be about 3 inches (8 cm) wide and 2.5 inches (6 cm) tall. Cut the lips out.
2. Press the red gemstone strips along the bottom edge of the poster board shape. Be careful to follow the shape of the lips.
3. Continue covering the lips with gemstones, working from the outside edge into the center. Leave the center empty.
4. Press on a line of pearls in the center to make teeth.
5. Turn the project over, and hot glue the pin to the back.

TOGETHER, SCHIAPARELLI AND DALI CREATED SOME MEMORABLE CLOTHES.

The humorous surreal style was often an illusion. Schiaparelli popularized the style called trompe l'oeil, which creates a 3D effect in clothing. Schiaparelli herself first turned heads by wearing a tromp l'oeil sweater. It looked like it had a real bow tied at the neck. But it was an illusion. The art was knitted into the sweater's design.

Trompe l'oeil fashions are still trendy. Paris Hilton, among other celebs, has pulled off this fashion magic. Designer Mary Katrantzou uses the style to make clothes that need no jewelry.

Together, Schiaparelli and Dali created some memorable clothes. Perhaps their most famous creations were the shoe hat and the lobster dress. Dali got the idea for the shoe hat when he put his wife's slipper on his head as a joke. The shoe hat looked exactly like a woman's very large black high heel worn upside down on the head.

The lobster dress was just that. It was a gorgeous full-length gown with a lobster printed on the front. By today's standards, the dress isn't very outrageous. But in the 1930s, it was a head-turning fashion statement.

Get the Look

Of course every stylish woman needs gloves to go with her shoe hat. Schiaparelli's gloves came with fingernails attached to the fingers. You can re-create those famous gloves.

SUPPLIES

- elbow-length satin gloves in whatever color you want
- press-on nails (Go for something wild!)

1. Your gloves probably came with cardboard inserts in them. Leave those inside while you do the project.
2. Follow the directions on your nail set to glue the nails in place over the glove's fingers.
3. Carefully take the cardboard out of the glove. Then do the other one.

chiaparelli's designs caught the attention of some big Hollywood stars. Celebrities such as Joan Crawford and Greta Garbo were her clients. Mae West had Schiaparelli design clothes for her movies.

Schiaparelli's surreal designs were even worn by one of the most famous women in the world. Wallis Simpson, who later married King Edward of Great Britain, enjoyed Schiaparelli's unusual clothing. Simpson is the person who actually wore Schiaparelli's and Dali's lobster gown.

Get the *Look*

Make a wild statement like Schiaperelli's and Dali's lobster dress. Be daring or just a bit wacky.

SUPPLIES:

- scissors
- 8½ x 11-inch (22 x 28-cm) piece of craft foam
- hot glue gun and glue
- pencil
- paper
- a clean peanut butter jar lid
- wax paper
- fabric paint in a complimentary color to your garment
- a solid colored dress, T-shirt, or jacket

1. Cut the craft foam in half, and glue the two halves together.
2. Sketch or find a picture of a crab, snail, or other interesting creature. The picture needs to be small enough to fit on top of the lid.
3. Trace your picture onto wax paper and cut it out.
4. Place the wax paper shape on the craft foam and trace around it.
5. Cut out the shape through the double-thickness of foam. Glue this foam shape to the outside of the lid.
6. Pour a little fabric paint onto a piece of wax paper. Dunk your stamp into the paint. Stamp the image onto your garment. Be creative and have fun! You could have a whole line of crabs marching up one side.

Since the days of Dali and Schiaparelli, designers have worked surreal ideas into their lines. As you can see, contemporary surreal fashion has come a long way.

In 2008 Viktor & Rolf released ready-to-wear coats that made a statement.

Agatha Ruiz de la Prada debuted a whimsical line of surreal fashion at the 2009 Milan Fashion week.

odern music stars have taken surreal styles to the extreme. In 2001 Björk wore the now famous swan dress to the Oscars. In 2008 Katy Perry wore Manish Arora's carousel dress. Nicki Minaj is always pushing the limits of fashion. And you can't forget Madonna's cone bra of the 1980s. But Lady Gaga might be the leader of the surreal pack. Her wearable art styles are often shocking, daring, and sometimes hard to look at. In 2010 Lady Gaga wore a dress made of raw meat. She said that dress sent the message that she has rights and is "not a piece of meat."

Next time someone wears a meat dress or a carousel dress, remember that's a 1930s fashion throwback.

Wearing Surreal *Fashion*

If surreal fashions sound more like art than clothing, that is the idea. Schiaparelli once said, "Dress designing, incidentally, is to me not a profession but an art."

Surreal styles are everywhere today. From funny sayings or pictures on T-shirts to animal heads for hats, many teens enjoy surreal styles.

Surreal styles are everywhere today.

JESSICA LU ACTRESS

ASHLEY TISDALE ACTRESS

"DRESS DESIGNING, INCIDENTALLY, IS TO ME NOT A PROFESSION BUT AN ART."

PUT IT TOGETHER

Give a nod to Schiaparelli and Dali with these surreal styles.

Surreal styles are hot trends. Accessory and department stores carry all kinds of pieces that will make you laugh.

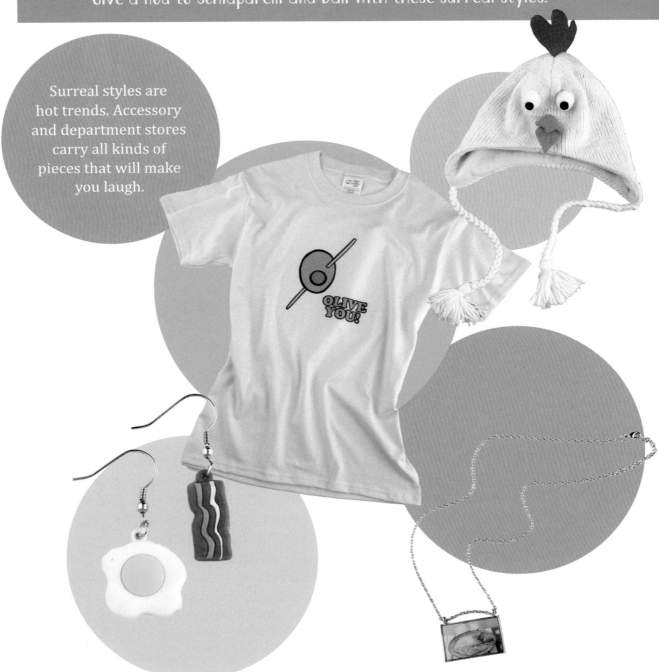

OLIVE YOU!

WEARING THE PROOF

Fashion trends of the 1920s and 1930s don't just live as memories in Great-Grandma's attic. These looks left a lasting imprint on fashion. No longer are women tightly corseted and covered past the ankles. The flapper dresses of the '20s lifted hems and gave women freedom.

The 1930's form fitting gowns celebrated the feminine body. Separates and masculine styles gave women choices. And surrealism gave people the chance to be shocking.

Because of the '20s and '30s, modern women have a style that merges beauty, fun, comfort, and freedom. Just look in your closet for the proof.

'20s AND '30s LOOKS LEFT A LASTING IMPRINT ON FASHION.

Glossary

bias cut (BYE-uhs CUT)—a way of cutting fabric that is diagonal to the grain of the fabric

corset (KOR-set)—a fitted undergarment used to give women a fashionable figure

fringe (FRINJ)—a border of cords or threads attached to something

hem (HEM)—a border of a cloth garment that is doubled back and stitched down

snood (SNOOD)—a net or fabric bag pinned or tied on at the back of a woman's head for holding hair

surrealism (suh-REE-uh-li-zuhm)—a style of art in which scenes show ordinary objects in unusual or unexpected ways; sometimes described as "dreamlike"

trompe l'oeil (tromp-LAY)—an artistic style where objects are drawn or made with realistic detail to trick the eye

Read More

Behnke, Alison Marie. *The Little Black Dress and Zoot Suits: Depression and Wartime Fashions from the 1930s to 1950s.* Dressing a Nation—The History of U.S. Fashion. Minneapolis: Twenty-First Century Books, 2012.

Luster, Lori. *Cool Cat: Bringing 1940s and 1950s Flare to Your Wardrobe.* Fashion Forward. North Mankato, Minn.: Capstone Press, 2014.

Niven, Felicia Lowenstein. *Fabulous Fashions of the 1930s.* Fabulous Fashions of the Decades. Berkeley Heights, N.J.: Enslow Publishers Inc., 2012.

Internet Sites

FactHound offers a safe, fun way to find Internet sites related to this book. All of the sites on FactHound have been researched by our staff.

Here's all you do:

Visit *www.facthound.com*

Type in this code: 9781476539973

 Super-cool stuff! Check out projects, games and lots more at **www.capstonekids.com**

Index